HOW IT HAPPENS
at the Pizza Company

By Shawndra Shofner
Photographs by Bob and Diane Wolfe

CLARA
HOUSE
BOOKS

Minneapolis

Thanks to Sheryl, Mary, Lynn, and Karen. Your great sense of humor keeps me going—SS
The publisher would like to thank Bernatello's and its employees for their generous help with this book.
All photographs by Bob and Diane Wolfe except p. 1 and back cover (Bernatello's).

Clara House Books
The Oliver Press, Inc.
Charlotte Square
5707 West 36th Street
Minneapolis, MN 55416-2510

Library of Congress Cataloging-in-Publication Data
Shofner, Shawndra.
    How it happens at the pizza company / by Shawndra Shofner ;
photographs by Bob and Diane Wolfe.
        p. cm.
    Includes index.
    ISBN 1-881508-98-6
  1. Pizza–Juvenile literature. 2. Pizza industry–Juvenile
literature. I. Title. II. Title: At the pizza company.
    TX770.P58S36 2006
    641.8'248–dc22

                                                    2006021827

ISBN 1-881508-98-6
Printed in the United States of America
10 09 08 07   8 7 6 5 4 3 2 1

This bubbling pepperoni pizza with its crispy crust, spicy-sweet sauce, and melted cheese was in the freezer less than fifteen minutes ago. Frozen pizza bakes quickly, is inexpensive, and tastes delicious. In fact, pizza is the hottest selling frozen food in the world. People eat more than a billion every year. Come along! See how one company makes more than 100,000 pizzas every day.

Mozzarella

Cheddar

Shredded Blend

Red & Green
Pepper & Onion

Sauce

Mushrooms

Pepperoni

Black Olives

Crust

Italian Sausage

INGREDIENTS

Every pizza this company makes starts with three main **ingredients**: a round crust, sauce, and cheese. Workers create many different kinds of pizzas by adding toppings such as red and green peppers, onions, pepperoni, sausage, mushrooms, and black olives.

A two-story tall cooler holds large quantities of fresh ingredients. Like your refrigerator at home, its temperature is a chilly 38 degrees Fahrenheit (3° C) to keep the foods from spoiling. When an ingredient is needed, a worker drives a forklift into the cooler. The cooler is organized so that the worker knows exactly where to go to get the ingredient.

SAUCE

Tomato paste, made from crushed tomatoes, is the main ingredient in sauce. Here, a worker opens a **tote**, or plastic-lined wooden box, of tomato paste. The tote weighs almost 3,000 pounds (1.3 mt)! There are more than 14,000 tomatoes in one tote of paste. This company uses three or four totes a day.

Black Pepper

Bernatello's
Spice Blend

Onion Powder

Salt

Basil

Oregano

Granulated
Garlic

Spices such as salt, black pepper, onion powder, basil, oregano, and garlic add zip to pizza sauce. This company uses a **blend** of these spices that gives their sauce a special flavor.

A machine forces tomato paste from the tote to a big mixing tub. A worker pours in one 15-pound (6.8 kg) bag of blended spices. Large beaters mix the paste and spices for 15 minutes. The sauce is ready. It is time to make pizza!

CRUST

This worker places crusts on cardboard circles. The stiff cardboard keeps the crusts from bending. From here, moving belts carry the crusts to the sauce machine.

Sauce travels from the mixing tank through
overhead pipes to the sauce machine. This machine
squirts hundreds of cone-shaped dots of sauce on the
crusts as they pass under it.

CHEESE

The sauce-covered crusts are ready for cheese. This company uses two kinds. One is a mild, white cheese called mozzarella. It comes in big blocks that weigh 10 pounds (4.5 kg) each—enough to top 40 pizzas! Cheddar is the other cheese. It's orange and tastes tangy.

Mozzarella

Cheddar

Shredded Blend

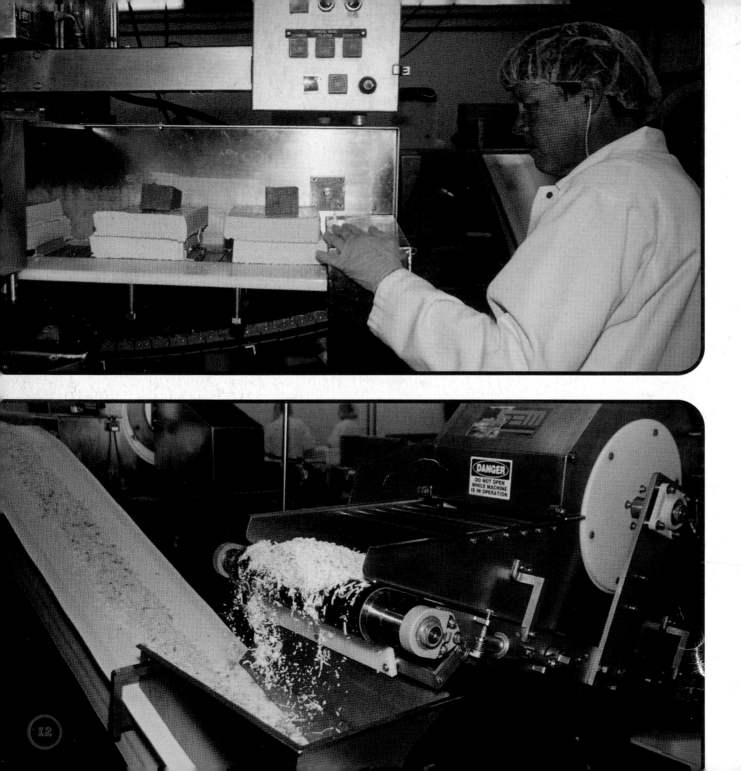

This worker loads mozzarella and cheddar into a machine that shreds the cheese.

Shredded cheese drops onto a wide belt. The belt carries the cheese to the sprinkling machine.

DANGER
DO NOT OPEN
WHILE MACHINE
IS IN OPERATION

Cheese sprinkles like a waterfall on the sauce-covered crusts. No cheese is wasted. Shreds that miss the pizzas fall onto another belt that returns them to the sprinkling machine.

PEPPERONI

Pepperoni is the most popular pizza topping in the world. Here, a worker cuts four-pound pepperoni sticks in half so they are easier to handle. He wears a safety glove to protect his hand.

The worker places the pepperoni sticks into holes on a plastic slicing guide. A blade cuts thin slices of pepperoni that evenly drop onto the pizzas.

Workers stand by to rearrange pepperoni slices that are out of place. They also replace end pieces.

LABELING AND WRAPPING

Now the pizzas must be labeled and wrapped. On the top of each pizza, a machine places a label that shows its brand name and a picture of its toppings.

The next machine takes plastic film from a large roll and forms a loose bag around each pizza.

Pizzas travel through a heated tunnel where the temperature is just warm enough to make the plastic bag shrink, but not cook the pizza. When the plastic bag shrinks, it makes a tightly sealed package around the pizza. After that, another machine sticks a label containing a list of ingredients and cooking directions to the underside of the package.

A scale weighs each pizza as it comes down the conveyor belt. If a pizza weighs less than what its label states, the machine pushes it off the belt. The pizza company wants to make sure that customers get exactly what they pay for.

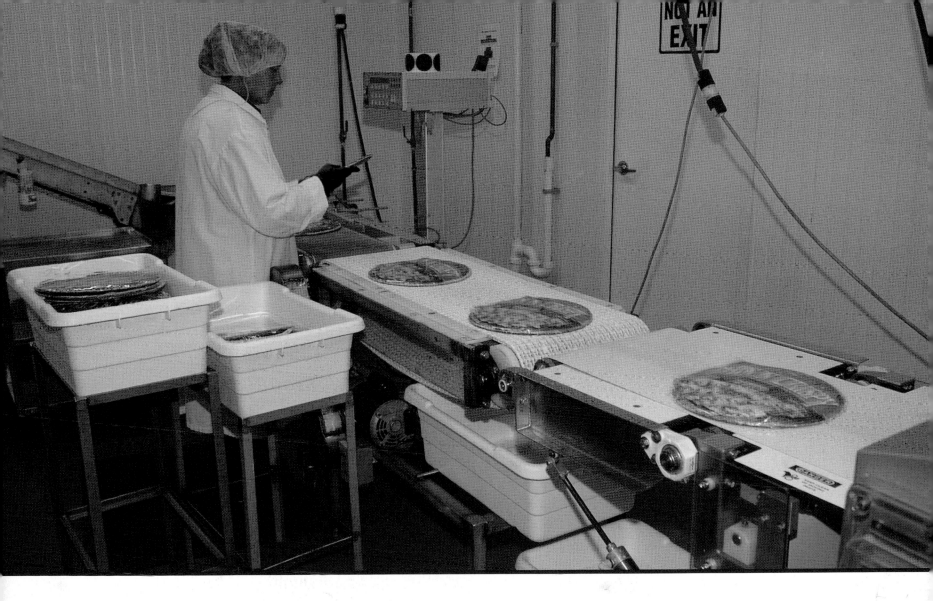

At final inspection, a worker makes sure the pizza, the labels, and the wrapper are all in the right place. If everything is not just right, the worker will set the pizza aside for repackaging.

If a pizza is underweight, it is removed from the line and fixed by hand. This worker is adding more cheese to increase the pizza's weight.

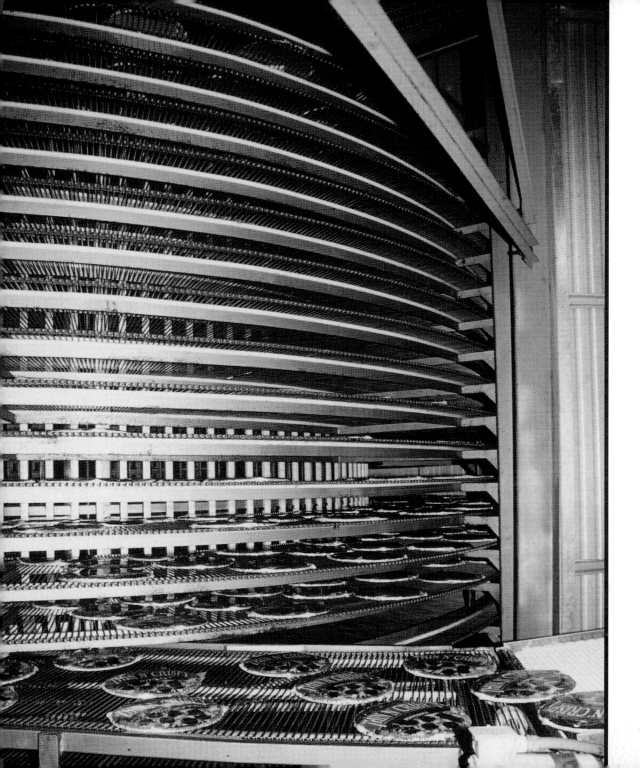

FREEZING

For the next 30 minutes, pizzas slowly turn up and around the inside of a spiral freezer. Its wind chill reaches -50 degrees Fahrenheit (- 45.5° C). This icy breeze freezes the pizzas fast and keeps them as fresh as the minute they were made.

PACKAGING

From the spiral freezer, pizzas slide down a twisting chute that looks like a playground slide. Another moving belt takes the pizzas to the packaging area.

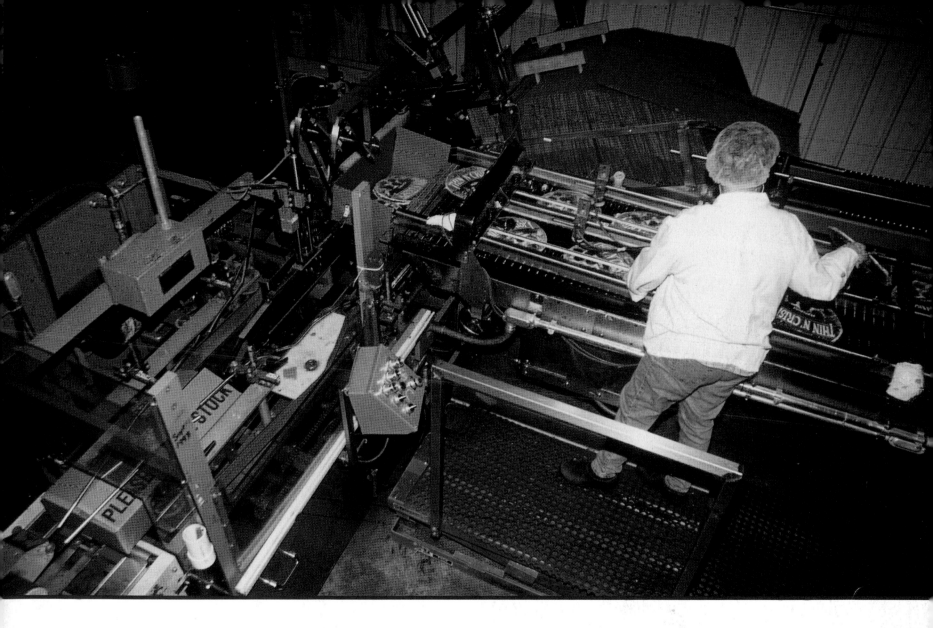

This machine counts 12 pizzas, slides them into a shipping box, and seals it. A worker makes sure that the pizzas fill the boxes evenly.

The boxes are taped shut after they've been filled and are then moved to a machine that stacks them.

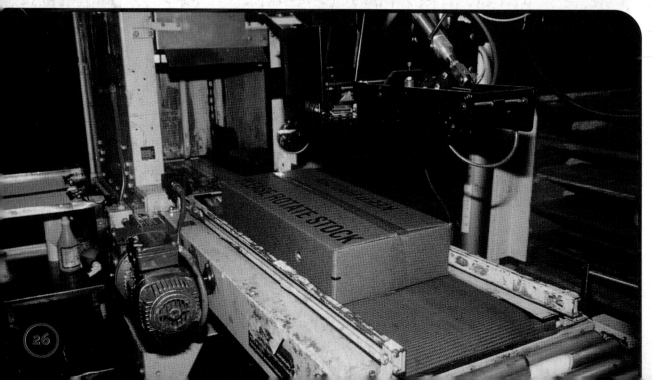

Wearing a snowsuit to stay warm, a worker drives a forklift carrying a pallet of boxes into the freezer. Packaged pizzas are stored in the drive-in freezer until the company needs to ship them to customers.

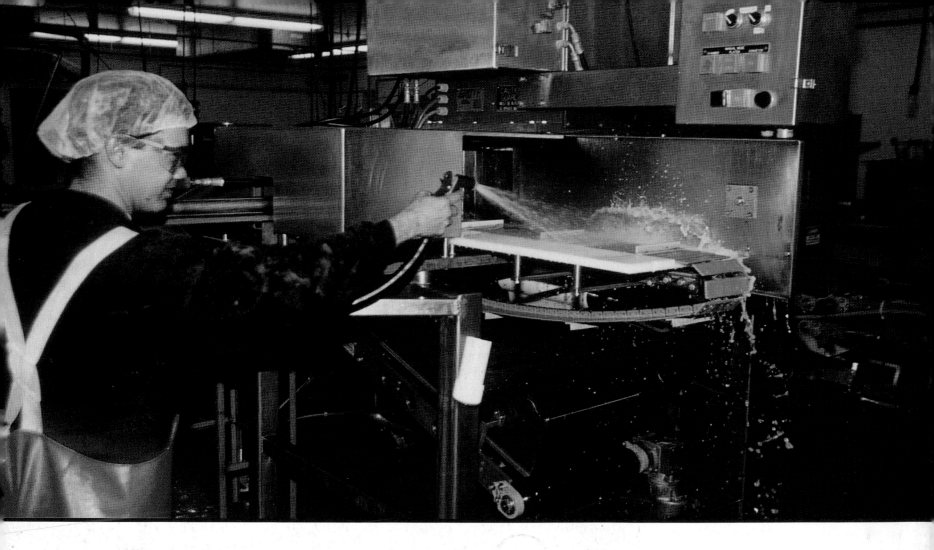

CLEAN-UP

This company shuts down all of its machines every night to clean and sanitize them. Clean-up takes about eight hours. Workers wash every piece of equipment with a foam cleaner that kills germs. They rinse the cleaner off with hot water and let the equipment air dry.

SHIPPING

Large and small trucks ship thousands of pizzas from this company every day. A forklift driver collects the boxes of pizza and drives them to a loading dock. Then, he and another worker wrap tall stacks of boxes in plastic to keep them from tipping over.

Workers load the boxes inside a truck. A **refrigeration unit** blows cold air inside the truck so the pizzas stay frozen on their way to the grocery store.

At the grocery store, the pizzas are unpacked and displayed in a freezer case so customers can buy them for a quick, inexpensive, delicious meal.

Glossary

blend: a mixture, as in a combination of spices

ingredients: items called for in a recipe

refrigeration unit: a machine that blows cold air inside a trailer

tomato paste: a thick food made from crushed tomatoes

tote: a 3,000-pound (1.3 mt) tomato paste container that is lined with plastic

Index

Websites

Bernatello's Pizza Company: www.bernatellos.com
Pizza Marketing Quarterly: www.pmq.com